Baby's First Year: A Comprehensive Guide for New Parents

Everything You Need to Know to Thrive in Your First Year as a Parent

BY

SENNETT HOWARD

CONTENTS

INTRODUCTION

Congratulations! Welcome to Parenthood, the most rewarding journey of your life. As you embark on this adventure, filled with love, joy, and a touch of chaos, this guide aims to provide you with the support and information you need to navigate the first year of your baby's life with confidence and ease.

Becoming a parent is a transformative experience, one

that brings immense joy and fulfillment but also challenges and uncertainties. From the moment you hold your precious newborn in your arms, you are entrusted with the extraordinary responsibility of nurturing and guiding them through the early stages of life. It's a journey filled with wonder, excitement, and endless learning opportunities.

Setting Realistic Expectations

One of the most important things to remember as a new parent is to set realistic expectations for yourself, your partner, and your baby. While parenthood is filled with moments of pure bliss, it also comes with its fair share of challenges and adjustments. Understanding that not every day will be perfect and that it's okay to ask for help when you need it can make all the difference in your journey.

It's essential to recognize that every baby is unique, and there is no one-size-fits-all approach to parenting. Your baby may not meet every milestone exactly on schedule, and that's perfectly normal. Instead of comparing your child to others, focus on celebrating their individual growth and development.

Parenthood is a marathon, not a sprint. Pace yourself, and remember that it's okay to prioritize your own well-being alongside your baby's needs. Take each day as it comes, and don't be too hard on yourself if things don't go according to plan. With patience, perseverance, and a healthy dose of humor, you'll navigate the challenges of the first year with grace and resilience.

Importance of Self-Care

Amidst the whirlwind of feedings, diaper changes, and sleepless nights, it's easy for new parents to neglect their own needs. However, self-care is crucial for your physical, emotional, and mental well-being, allowing you to be the best parent possible for your baby.

Make time for yourself, even if it's just a few minutes each day. Whether it's taking a relaxing bath, going for a walk, or indulging in your favorite hobby, prioritizing self-care will help you recharge and stay resilient in the face of challenges.

Remember that self-care isn't selfish — it's necessary. By taking care of yourself, you're better able to show up fully for your baby and your family. So don't feel guilty about taking time for yourself; consider it an essential part of your parenting toolkit.

Building a Support System

They say it takes a village to raise a child, and it's true. Surrounding yourself with a strong support system can make all the difference in your parenting journey. Whether it's friends who lend a listening ear, family members who offer practical assistance, or fellow parents who understand what you're going through, having a support network in place can provide comfort and reassurance during both the good times and the tough times.

Reach out to other parents in your community through parenting groups, classes, or online forums. Sharing experiences, tips, and advice can help you feel less alone and more empowered as you navigate the ups and downs of parenthood together.

Don't hesitate to lean on your partner for support as well. Parenthood is a team effort, and having open communication and a strong partnership can help alleviate stress and strengthen your bond as a family. Remember, you're in this together, and by supporting each other, you'll emerge stronger and more connected than ever before.

Embracing the Journey Ahead

As you embark on this incredible journey of parenthood, remember to cherish each moment and embrace the beauty of the present. Your baby's first year will be filled with countless milestones, from their first smile to their first steps, and everything in between. Take the time to savor these precious moments and create lasting memories with your little one.

While there will inevitably be challenges along the way, know that you are capable, resilient, and deeply loved by your child. Trust your instincts, lean on your support system, and remember that there is no greater privilege than being a parent. Welcome to the adventure of a lifetime—get ready for a year filled with love, laughter, and endless possibilities.

In the pages that follow, we'll delve into the practical aspects of caring for your newborn, from feeding and sleep to development and health. Armed with knowledge, support, and a whole lot of love, you'll be well-equipped to navigate the joys and challenges of your baby's first year with confidence and grace. So let's dive in and embark on this incredible journey together. Parenthood awaits!

Chapter 01

Preparing for Baby's Arrival

As you eagerly anticipate the arrival of your little one, it's essential to take the time to prepare your home and family for the exciting journey ahead. From creating a safe and comfortable nursery to stocking up on newborn essentials, this chapter will guide you through the process of getting ready for your baby's arrival.

Creating a Safe and Comfortable Nursery

Your baby's nursery will serve as their sanctuary—a place where they can rest, play, and grow. Creating a safe and comfortable environment is paramount for their well-being. Start by choosing a quiet and well-ventilated room for the nursery, preferably close to your own bedroom for convenience during nighttime feedings and comforting.

Ensure that the crib meets current safety standards, with slats no more than 2-3 inches apart to prevent the risk of entrapment. Invest in a firm mattress that fits snugly within the crib, along with fitted sheets designed specifically for cribs.

Consider the layout of the nursery, keeping essential items like the crib, changing table, and feeding chair easily accessible. Install baby-proofing measures such as outlet covers, cabinet locks, and corner guards to prevent accidents as your baby becomes more mobile.

Personalize the nursery with soothing colors, soft lighting, and comforting décor to create a nurturing atmosphere. Hang blackout curtains to promote better sleep and consider adding a white noise machine or soft music player to help soothe your baby to sleep.

Essential Baby Gear Checklist

Preparing for your baby's arrival involves gathering essential gear to make the transition to parenthood smoother and more manageable. While it's easy to feel overwhelmed by the sheer number of baby products available, focusing on the essentials can help streamline your shopping list.

Here's a checklist of must-have baby gear:

1. **Crib or Bassinet:** Provide a safe and comfortable sleeping space for your baby.

2. **Diapers and Wipes:** Stock up on newborn-sized diapers and plenty of wipes for diaper changes.

3. **Clothing:** Invest in a variety of onesies, sleepers, socks, hats, and swaddles to keep your baby cozy and comfortable.

4. **Feeding Supplies:** Whether you plan to breastfeed or bottle-feed, make sure you have the necessary supplies, including bottles, nipples, breast pumps, nursing pads, and formula (if needed).

5. **Car Seat:** Install a rear-facing car seat according to manufacturer guidelines to ensure your baby's safety during car rides.

6. **Stroller:** Choose a stroller that suits your lifestyle and needs, whether it's a lightweight umbrella stroller or a sturdy jogging stroller.

7. **Baby Carrier or Wrap:** Keep your baby close and your hands free with a comfortable baby carrier or wrap for on-the-go convenience.

8. **Diaper Bag:** Organize all your baby essentials for outings with a spacious and functional diaper bag.

9. **Health and Safety Items:** Stock a first-aid kit with baby-friendly supplies, along with a digital thermometer, infant nail clippers, and baby-safe sunscreen.

10. **Baby Monitor:** Stay connected to your baby's needs with a reliable baby monitor that offers audio and video monitoring capabilities.

Remember, you don't need to have everything right away. Focus on the essentials, and you can always add additional items as needed once your baby arrives.

Preparing Siblings and Pets for Baby

Welcoming a new addition to the family can be an exciting but also challenging time for siblings and pets. Help ease the transition by involving them in the preparations and gradually introducing them to the idea of a new family member.

Talk to your older children about the upcoming arrival of their new sibling, emphasizing the positive aspects of being a big brother or sister. Involve them in setting up the nursery, choosing baby names, and selecting baby clothes and toys.

Address any concerns or fears they may have about sharing your attention or feeling left out. Reassure them of your love and explain that while things may change, your bond as a family will only grow stronger with the new addition.

If you have pets, gradually acclimate them to the sights, sounds, and smells of a baby by bringing home items with baby scents, playing recordings of baby noises, and allowing them to explore baby gear like cribs and strollers.

Supervise interactions between pets and your baby, and always prioritize safety. Teach children how to interact gently and respectfully with pets, and never leave them unsupervised together.

Understanding Birth Plans and Labor Options

As you prepare for the birth of your baby, it's essential to consider your preferences and options regarding labor and delivery. A birth plan is a written document that outlines your preferences for how you'd like your birth experience to unfold, including pain management, labor positions, and interventions.

Discuss your birth plan with your healthcare provider to ensure that your wishes align with their practices and hospital policies. Keep in mind that flexibility is key, as labor and delivery can be unpredictable, and unexpected circumstances may arise.

Educate yourself about different labor options, including natural childbirth, medicated pain relief, and medical interventions such as epidurals and cesarean sections. Attend childbirth education classes or workshops to learn about the stages of labor, coping techniques, and breathing exercises to help you feel more prepared and confident during labor.

Remember that the most important thing is the safe arrival of your baby, so trust your instincts and advocate for yourself throughout the birthing process. Surround yourself with a supportive birth team, including your partner, doula, and healthcare provider, who will help guide you through this transformative experience with compassion and care.

Stocking Up on Newborn Essentials

In the final weeks of pregnancy, it's time to stock up on essential items to ensure you're fully prepared for your baby's arrival. Create a checklist of newborn essentials and start gathering supplies to make the transition to parenthood smoother and more manageable.

Here are some items to include on your newborn essentials checklist:

1. **Diapers and Wipes:** Stock up on newborn-sized diapers and plenty of wipes for diaper changes.

2. **Clothing:** Invest in a variety of onesies, sleepers, socks, hats, and swaddles to keep your baby cozy and comfortable.

3. **Feeding Supplies:** Whether you plan to breastfeed or bottle-feed, make sure you have the necessary supplies, including bottles, nipples, breast pumps, nursing pads, and formula (if needed).

4. **Bedding:** Ensure your baby has a safe and comfortable sleeping environment with a fitted crib sheet, waterproof mattress cover, and lightweight blankets for swaddling.

5. **Bathing Supplies:** Gather baby-friendly soap, shampoo, lotion, towels, and washcloths for gentle and soothing bath times.

6. **Health and Safety Items:** Stock a first-aid kit with baby-friendly supplies, along with a digital thermometer, infant nail clippers, and baby-safe sunscreen.

7. **Transportation Gear:** Install a rear-facing car seat according to manufacturer guidelines to ensure your baby's safety during car rides, and choose a stroller that suits your lifestyle and needs.

8. **Breastfeeding Support:** Consider investing in breastfeeding accessories such as nursing bras, nipple cream, and breast pads to make breastfeeding more comfortable and convenient.

By preparing your home, family, and self for your baby's

arrival, you can approach the birth with confidence and excitement. Remember to trust your instincts, stay flexible, and embrace the journey ahead with open arms. Parenthood is a remarkable adventure, and your baby's arrival will fill your life with immeasurable love, joy, and wonder. Get ready for the most incredible journey of your life — the journey of welcoming your precious little one into the world.

Chapter 02

The First Weeks at Home

The first weeks at home with your newborn are a whirlwind of emotions, adjustments, and precious moments. As you settle into your new role as parents, this chapter will guide you through the joys and challenges of the newborn phase, from sleepless nights to heartwarming cuddles.

Navigating the Newborn Phase: Sleep, Feeding, and Diapering

The newborn phase is characterized by round-the-clock care, as your baby adjusts to life outside the womb and you learn to respond to their needs. Sleep, feeding, and diapering will become central aspects of your daily routine.

Establishing a consistent sleep routine can help promote better sleep for both you and your baby. While newborns sleep for short periods throughout the day and night, aim to create a calming bedtime routine to signal to your baby that it's time to wind down. Keep the environment dark, quiet, and comfortable, and consider using white noise or gentle music to soothe your baby to sleep.

Feeding your newborn on demand is essential for their growth and development. Whether you choose to breastfeed or bottle-feed, pay attention to your baby's hunger cues and offer frequent feedings throughout the day and night. Keep track of feeding times and diaper changes to ensure your baby is getting enough nourishment and staying hydrated.

Diapering is another essential aspect of newborn care. Keep a supply of diapers, wipes, and diaper rash cream on hand, and change your baby's diaper frequently to prevent discomfort and irritation. Remember to clean the diaper area thoroughly and pat dry before applying diaper cream or putting on a fresh diaper.

Bonding with Baby: Skin-to-Skin Contact and Cuddle Time

Bonding with your baby is a precious and transformative experience that lays the foundation for a strong and secure attachment. Skin-to-skin contact, also known as kangaroo care, is a powerful way to bond with your baby and promote feelings of warmth, security, and connection.

Hold your baby against your bare chest, allowing them to feel the rhythm of your heartbeat and the warmth of your skin. Skin-to-skin contact has numerous benefits for both you and your baby, including regulating your baby's temperature, heart rate, and breathing, promoting breastfeeding success, and reducing stress for both of you.

In addition to skin-to-skin contact, make time for cuddle sessions throughout the day. Snuggle with your baby, sing lullabies, and engage in gentle touch to strengthen your bond and create lasting memories together. Remember, there's no such thing as holding your baby too much—responding to your baby's need for closeness and comfort is one of the most important ways you can nurture their emotional well-being.

Recognizing Newborn Cues and Needs

Understanding your newborn's cues and needs is key to providing responsive and attentive care. While newborns may not be able to communicate verbally, they use a variety of cues to convey their needs and emotions.

Pay attention to your baby's body language, facial expressions, and vocalizations to decipher what they're trying to tell you. Cues such as rooting, sucking motions, and hand-to-mouth movements may indicate hunger, while fussiness, crying, and arching of the back may signal discomfort or overstimulation.

Respond to your baby's cues promptly and with sensitivity, offering comfort, nourishment, or a change of environment as needed. Trust your instincts as a parent and don't be afraid to seek support or guidance if you're unsure how to respond to your baby's cues.

Managing Visitors and Setting Boundaries

In the early weeks after your baby's birth, it's natural for friends and family members to want to visit and meet the newest member of the family. While their excitement and support are appreciated, managing visitors and setting boundaries is essential for your well-being and your baby's.

Establish clear guidelines for visitors, including timing, duration, and health precautions such as hand washing and avoiding close contact if they're feeling unwell. Consider designating specific visiting hours or days to allow for rest and recovery without feeling overwhelmed by constant visitors.

Don't hesitate to communicate your needs and preferences to friends and family members, and don't feel obligated to entertain guests if you're feeling exhausted or overwhelmed. Your priority should be taking care of yourself and your baby, so prioritize rest, relaxation, and bonding time as needed.

Coping with Postpartum Emotions and Recovery

The postpartum period is a time of significant physical, emotional, and hormonal changes, often accompanied by a range of emotions including joy, anxiety, sadness, and overwhelm. Coping with postpartum emotions and recovery is a crucial aspect of adjusting to life with a newborn.

Reach out for support from your partner, family members, friends, or healthcare provider if you're struggling with postpartum emotions or feeling overwhelmed. Talking about your feelings, seeking reassurance, and receiving practical assistance can help alleviate stress and promote emotional well-being.

Prioritize self-care during the postpartum period, including rest, nourishing meals, gentle exercise, and activities that bring you joy and relaxation. Accept help from others and delegate tasks when possible, allowing you to focus on recovering from childbirth and bonding with your baby.

If you're experiencing symptoms of postpartum depression or anxiety, don't hesitate to seek professional help. Postpartum mood disorders are common and treatable, and getting the support you need is essential for your well-being and your ability to care for your baby.

By navigating the challenges and joys of the first weeks at home with intention and compassion, you'll lay a strong foundation for your journey as parents. Remember to prioritize self-care, trust your instincts, and cherish the precious moments with your newborn. Parenthood is a remarkable adventure, and the first weeks at home with your baby are just the beginning of a lifetime of love, learning, and growth.

Chapter 03

Feeding Your Baby

Feeding your baby is one of the most fundamental aspects of parenting, providing essential nourishment for their growth and development. Whether you choose to breastfeed, bottle-feed, or introduce solids, this chapter will guide you through the ins and outs of feeding your baby with confidence and ease.

Breastfeeding Basics: Latching, Positioning, and Establishing Supply

Breastfeeding is a natural and beautiful way to nourish your baby, offering numerous benefits for both you and your little one. To establish successful breastfeeding, it's essential to master the basics of latching, positioning, and establishing a good milk supply.

Ensure your baby is properly latched onto your breast, with their mouth covering both the nipple and a portion of the areola. A deep latch allows your baby to effectively extract milk and reduces the risk of nipple pain and discomfort.

Experiment with different breastfeeding positions to find what works best for you and your baby. Common positions include the cradle hold, cross-cradle hold, football hold, and side-lying position. Choose a comfortable and supportive chair or nursing pillow to help you maintain proper posture and reduce strain on your back and shoulders.

Establishing a healthy milk supply is crucial for successful breastfeeding. Nurse your baby frequently, aiming for 8-12 feedings per day in the early weeks.

Offer both breasts at each feeding to ensure your baby receives the hindmilk, which is richer in fat and calories.

Stay hydrated and nourished by drinking plenty of water and eating a balanced diet rich in fruits, vegetables, whole grains, and lean proteins. Get plenty of rest and relaxation to support your body's milk production and overall well-being.

Bottle Feeding: Choosing Formula and Feeding Techniques

While breastfeeding is often considered the ideal way to feed your baby, bottle feeding with formula is a perfectly valid and nutritious option for many families. If breastfeeding isn't possible or desired, choosing the right formula and mastering bottle feeding techniques can help ensure your baby receives the nourishment they need to thrive.

Select a formula that meets your baby's nutritional needs and any specific dietary considerations, such as cow's milk protein allergy or lactose intolerance. Opt for iron-fortified formulas, which provide essential nutrients for your baby's growth and development.

When bottle feeding, hold your baby in a semi-upright position to reduce the risk of ear infections and choking. Ensure the bottle nipple is filled with milk to prevent your baby from swallowing air, which can lead to gas and discomfort.

Offer the bottle in a calm and quiet environment,

avoiding distractions and allowing your baby to focus on feeding. Hold the bottle at a slight angle to prevent milk from flowing too quickly and overwhelming your baby.

Introducing Solids: Signs of Readiness and First Foods

As your baby approaches six months of age, they may be ready to start exploring solid foods alongside breast milk or formula. Look for signs of readiness, such as sitting up with support, showing interest in food, and exhibiting good head control and swallowing reflexes.

Begin with single-ingredient purees or mashed foods, such as cooked sweet potato, avocado, banana, or infant cereal mixed with breast milk or formula. Introduce one new food at a time, waiting several days before offering another to monitor for any signs of food allergies or sensitivities.

Gradually increase the variety and texture of foods as your baby grows and becomes more accustomed to eating solids. Offer a balanced diet that includes a variety of fruits, vegetables, grains, proteins, and healthy fats to support your baby's nutritional needs and palate development.

Handling Feeding Challenges: Reflux, Allergies, and Intolerances

Feeding challenges such as reflux, allergies, and intolerances are common among infants and can present unique obstacles for parents. Understanding the signs and symptoms of these conditions and knowing how to manage them can help alleviate discomfort and promote healthy feeding habits.

Reflux occurs when stomach contents flow back into the esophagus, causing spit-up or vomiting. Keep your baby upright after feedings, burp them frequently, and consider smaller, more frequent feedings to help reduce reflux symptoms.

Food allergies and intolerances can manifest as digestive issues, skin rashes, respiratory symptoms, or behavioral changes. If you suspect your baby has a food allergy or intolerance, consult with your pediatrician for evaluation and guidance on allergen avoidance and alternative feeding options.

Building Healthy Eating Habits for Baby's Future

Establishing healthy eating habits early in life lays the foundation for lifelong wellness and nutrition. Introduce a wide variety of flavors and textures to your baby from the start, encouraging them to explore and enjoy a diverse range of foods.

Lead by example by modeling healthy eating behaviors and offering nutritious meals and snacks as a family. Create a positive mealtime environment free from distractions and pressure, allowing your baby to eat at their own pace and listen to their hunger and fullness cues.

Avoid using food as a reward or punishment and refrain from pressuring your baby to eat more than they desire. Trust your baby's innate ability to self-regulate their food intake and honor their preferences and appetite as they grow and develop.

By prioritizing your baby's nutritional needs and fostering a positive feeding relationship, you'll set the stage for a lifetime of healthy eating habits and enjoyment of food. Embrace the journey of feeding your baby with love, patience, and joy, knowing that you're nourishing their body, mind, and spirit with every bite.

Chapter 04

Baby's Development Milestones

As your baby grows and explores the world around them, they'll reach a series of developmental milestones that mark their progress and achievements. From their first smile to their first steps, this chapter will guide you through tracking, encouraging, and celebrating your baby's development.

Tracking Baby's Growth and Development

Tracking your baby's growth and development is an essential part of parenting, allowing you to monitor their progress and identify any areas of concern. Keep track of key milestones in areas such as motor skills, language development, social interaction, and cognitive abilities.

Use a growth chart provided by your pediatrician to monitor your baby's height, weight, and head circumference over time. Plotting these measurements on a growth chart can help ensure your baby is growing at a healthy rate and identify any potential growth concerns.

In addition to physical growth, keep an eye on your baby's developmental milestones, such as:

Motor Skills: Rolling over, sitting up, crawling, standing, and walking.
Language Development: Babbling, cooing, saying first words, and understanding simple commands.
Social Interaction: Smiling, making eye contact, responding to familiar faces, and engaging in interactive play.

Cognitive Abilities: Exploring objects with hands and mouth, recognizing familiar objects and faces, and demonstrating problem-solving skills.

Keep a journal or milestone tracker to record your baby's developmental milestones, from their first smile and coo to their first words and steps. Take photos and videos to capture these precious moments and create lasting memories of your baby's journey.

Encouraging Tummy Time and Motor Skills Development

Tummy time is a crucial activity for your baby's development, helping to strengthen their neck, shoulder, and arm muscles and promote motor skills development. Start tummy time from birth, placing your baby on their stomach for short periods several times a day, gradually increasing the duration as they grow older.

Provide a firm and comfortable surface for tummy time, such as a play mat or blanket on the floor. Engage your baby with toys, mirrors, and colorful objects to encourage reaching, grasping, and exploring during tummy time.

As your baby grows and develops, support their motor skills development through activities such as crawling, rolling, sitting, and eventually standing and walking. Offer age-appropriate toys and activities that stimulate their curiosity and encourage movement and exploration.

Encourage your baby to explore their environment and interact with objects of varying textures, shapes, and sizes. Provide opportunities for sensory stimulation through activities such as playing with water, sand, or play dough, and exploring different sounds and music.

Stimulating Baby's Senses through Play and Interaction

Babies learn about the world around them through their senses, so it's essential to provide opportunities for sensory stimulation and exploration through play and interaction. Engage your baby's senses of sight, hearing, touch, taste, and smell with a variety of stimulating activities and experiences.

Use high-contrast black and white images or brightly colored toys to capture your baby's attention and encourage visual development. Sing songs, play music, and make sounds to stimulate your baby's hearing and promote language development.

Provide a variety of textures for your baby to touch and explore, from soft blankets and plush toys to textured balls and sensory bins filled with rice or water. Offer safe objects for your baby to mouth and explore, supporting their oral sensory development and teething.

Understanding Developmental Red Flags and When to Seek Help

While every baby develops at their own pace, it's essential to be aware of developmental red flags that may indicate potential concerns or delays. Keep an eye out for signs such as limited eye contact, delayed motor milestones, difficulty responding to sounds or voices, and lack of interest in social interaction.

Trust your instincts as a parent and don't hesitate to consult with your pediatrician if you have any concerns about your baby's development. Early intervention is key to addressing developmental delays and providing support and resources to help your baby reach their full potential.

Keep in mind that developmental milestones are guidelines, not strict deadlines. Every baby is unique and may reach milestones at their own pace. However, if you notice significant delays or regression in your baby's development, it's important to seek professional evaluation and support.

Celebrating Each Milestone, Big or Small

Every milestone, big or small, is cause for celebration in your baby's journey of growth and development. Whether it's their first smile, first laugh, or first steps, take the time to acknowledge and celebrate these achievements with joy and pride.

Create a milestone board or journal to document your baby's milestones and accomplishments, along with photos and notes commemorating each special moment. Share these milestones with friends and family members to spread the joy and excitement of your baby's achievements.

Celebrate your baby's milestones with special activities or treats, such as a family outing, a favorite meal, or a small gift to mark the occasion. Take plenty of photos and videos to capture these precious moments and create lasting memories of your baby's journey.

Remember that every baby is unique, and developmental milestones may vary from child to child. Focus on your baby's individual progress and celebrate their strengths and abilities, knowing that each step forward is a testament to their resilience, curiosity, and spirit.

By tracking, encouraging, and celebrating your baby's development milestones, you'll support their growth and learning in meaningful ways. Embrace the journey of parenthood with wonder and gratitude, knowing that you're guiding your baby toward a future filled with endless possibilities and opportunities for growth.

Chapter 05

Establishing Routines and Sleep Patterns

The journey of establishing routines and sleep patterns for your baby is both a challenging and rewarding aspect of parenthood. This chapter aims to provide a comprehensive guide to help you navigate through this journey with confidence, covering various topics such as creating consistent bedtime routines, understanding your baby's sleep needs and cycles, implementing safe sleep practices, managing sleep challenges, and supporting healthy sleep habits for the whole family.

Creating a Consistent Bedtime Routine

A consistent bedtime routine serves as a crucial anchor for your baby, signaling the transition from wakefulness to sleep. Establishing a predictable sequence of calming activities helps your baby relax and unwind, setting the stage for a restful night's sleep.

Begin your bedtime routine about 30 to 60 minutes before your baby's anticipated bedtime. Consistency is key, so aim to follow the same sequence of activities each night, even when traveling or during times of disruption.

Choose soothing activities that promote relaxation and prepare your baby for sleep. These may include a warm bath, gentle massage, soft music or lullabies, cuddling with a favorite blanket or stuffed animal, and reading a bedtime story.

Dim the lights and create a calm and peaceful environment to encourage relaxation. Minimize stimulating activities such as screen time or rough play, as these can interfere with your baby's ability to settle down and fall asleep.

Understanding Baby's Sleep Cycles and Needs

Understanding your baby's sleep cycles and needs is essential for promoting healthy sleep habits and addressing any sleep challenges that may arise. Newborns have shorter sleep cycles than adults, typically lasting 50 to 60 minutes, and spend more time in active REM (rapid eye movement) sleep.

As your baby grows and develops, their sleep patterns will gradually mature, with longer periods of deep sleep and more consolidated nighttime sleep. By around three to six months of age, many babies begin to develop a more predictable sleep schedule with longer stretches of nighttime sleep.

Keep in mind that every baby is unique, and sleep patterns can vary widely from child to child. Pay attention to your baby's individual sleep cues and preferences, and adjust your routines and expectations accordingly.

Implementing Safe Sleep Practices: SIDS Prevention

Safe sleep practices are crucial for reducing the risk of Sudden Infant Death Syndrome (SIDS) and creating a safe sleeping environment for your baby. Follow the

American Academy of Pediatrics (AAP) guidelines for safe sleep, which include:

- Placing your baby on their back to sleep, both for naps and nighttime sleep.
- Using a firm and flat sleep surface, such as a crib mattress with a fitted sheet.
- Avoiding soft bedding, pillows, blankets, stuffed animals, or crib bumpers in your baby's sleep area.
- Keeping your baby's sleep area free from hazards such as loose cords, wires, or dangling window blinds.
- Sharing a room with your baby, but not a bed, for the first six to 12 months of life.

By following these guidelines, you can create a safe sleep environment that reduces the risk of SIDS and promotes optimal sleep for your baby.

Handling Sleep Challenges: Night Wakings and Sleep Regression

Despite your best efforts, sleep challenges such as night wakings and sleep regression may occur at various stages of your baby's development. Understanding the underlying causes of these challenges and implementing strategies to address them can help you navigate these rough patches with confidence.

Night wakings are a normal part of infant sleep and may occur due to hunger, discomfort, teething, or developmental milestones. Respond to your baby's needs promptly and with sensitivity, offering comfort, reassurance, and nourishment as needed.

If your baby experiences a sleep regression, such as increased night wakings or difficulty settling down for sleep, remember that it's often temporary and part of their natural development. Stick to your established bedtime routine, offer extra comfort and support, and be patient as your baby adjusts to the changes.

Supporting Healthy Sleep Habits for the Whole Family

Promoting healthy sleep habits extends beyond your baby to include the entire family. Prioritize your own sleep and well-being by establishing a consistent bedtime routine and creating a sleep-friendly environment for yourself.

Practice good sleep hygiene habits, such as avoiding caffeine and electronic devices before bedtime, maintaining a comfortable sleep environment, and practicing relaxation techniques such as deep breathing or meditation to promote restful sleep.

Communicate openly with your partner about your sleep needs and share responsibilities for nighttime caregiving and soothing. Consider taking turns with nighttime feedings and wake-ups to ensure both parents have the opportunity for adequate rest and recovery.

By prioritizing healthy sleep habits for the whole family, you'll create a supportive and nurturing environment that promotes optimal sleep and well-being for everyone.

Conclusion

Establishing routines and sleep patterns for your baby is a journey filled with ups and downs, challenges and rewards. By creating a consistent bedtime routine, understanding your baby's sleep needs and cycles, implementing safe sleep practices, managing sleep challenges, and supporting healthy sleep habits for the whole family, you'll lay the foundation for a lifetime of restful nights and happy days.

Remember to be patient and flexible as you navigate the twists and turns of parenthood. Cherish the quiet moments of snuggles and cuddles, and celebrate the milestones, big and small, along the way. Parenthood is a remarkable journey, and with love, patience, and perseverance, you'll navigate the challenges of sleep and routines with grace and confidence.

Chapter 06

Nurturing Baby's Health and Wellness

Ensuring your baby's health and wellness is a top priority for every parent. This chapter is dedicated to providing comprehensive guidance on nurturing your baby's physical and emotional well-being, covering topics such as scheduling well-baby checkups and vaccinations, recognizing signs of illness, practicing good hygiene, building a strong immune system, and exploring holistic approaches to healthcare.

Scheduling Well-Baby Checkups and Vaccinations

Regular well-baby checkups are essential for monitoring your baby's growth and development and addressing any health concerns in a timely manner. These appointments typically occur at regular intervals during the first year of life, with additional visits scheduled as needed.

During well-baby checkups, your pediatrician will assess your baby's growth, development, and overall health, and provide guidance on feeding, sleep, safety, and immunizations. These appointments also offer an opportunity to discuss any questions or concerns you may have about your baby's health and well-being.

Vaccinations are a critical component of protecting your baby against serious and potentially life-threatening diseases. Following the recommended vaccination schedule provided by your pediatrician helps ensure your baby receives timely protection against illnesses such as measles, mumps, rubella, polio, and whooping cough.

Recognizing Signs of Illness and When to Call the Pediatrician

As a parent, it's essential to be vigilant and attentive to your baby's health, recognizing signs of illness and knowing when to seek medical attention. While some symptoms may be harmless and resolve on their own, others may indicate a more serious underlying condition.

Common signs of illness in babies include fever, coughing, sneezing, congestion, difficulty breathing, vomiting, diarrhea, rash, lethargy, irritability, and poor feeding. Trust your instincts as a parent and don't hesitate to contact your pediatrician if you have any concerns about your baby's health.

In some cases, prompt medical attention may be necessary to address a serious illness or infection. Seek immediate medical care if your baby experiences symptoms such as difficulty breathing, persistent vomiting or diarrhea, seizures, excessive lethargy, or signs of dehydration.

Practicing Good Hygiene and Preventing Common Infections

Practicing good hygiene is essential for preventing the spread of common infections and keeping your baby healthy. Follow these simple tips to maintain a clean and hygienic environment for your baby:

- Wash your hands frequently with soap and water, especially before handling your baby, preparing food, or feeding.
- Keep your baby's environment clean and sanitized, regularly disinfecting surfaces, toys, and other frequently touched items.
- Practice proper respiratory hygiene by covering your mouth and nose with a tissue or your elbow when coughing or sneezing.
- Avoid exposing your baby to sick individuals and crowded or enclosed spaces where the risk of infection is higher.

Breastfeed your baby if possible, as breast milk provides antibodies and nutrients that help protect against infections.

Building Baby's Immune System: Nutrition and Environment

Building a strong immune system is essential for protecting your baby against infections and promoting overall health and wellness. Support your baby's immune system through nutrition, environmental factors, and lifestyle choices:

- Breastfeeding provides essential nutrients and antibodies that help strengthen your baby's immune system and protect against infections. Aim to breastfeed exclusively for the first six months of life, if possible, and continue breastfeeding alongside complementary foods for at least the first year.
- Introduce a variety of nutritious foods into your

baby's diet, including fruits, vegetables, whole grains, lean proteins, and healthy fats. These foods provide essential vitamins, minerals, and antioxidants that support immune function and overall health.

- Ensure your baby receives adequate sleep and restorative rest, as sleep plays a crucial role in immune function and recovery from illness. Establish a consistent bedtime routine and create a sleep-friendly environment to promote healthy sleep habits.

- Provide opportunities for physical activity and exploration, as regular exercise helps support immune function and overall well-being. Engage in age-appropriate activities that encourage movement, play, and sensory exploration.

Exploring Holistic Approaches to Baby's Health Care

In addition to conventional medical care, many parents are interested in exploring holistic approaches to their baby's health and wellness. Holistic healthcare focuses on treating the whole person—body, mind, and spirit— and considers factors such as nutrition, lifestyle, environment, and emotional well-being.

Holistic approaches to baby's health care may include:

- **Chiropractic care:** Gentle spinal adjustments and manipulations to promote alignment, alleviate discomfort, and support overall health and well-being.
- **Acupuncture and acupressure:** Traditional Chinese

medicine techniques that involve stimulating specific points on the body to promote balance, relieve symptoms, and support healing.

- **Herbal remedies:** Natural remedies such as herbal teas, tinctures, and supplements that may offer immune support, digestive relief, or symptom relief for common ailments.
- **Massage therapy:** Gentle massage techniques to promote relaxation, improve circulation, relieve tension, and support bonding between parent and baby.

Before exploring holistic approaches to your baby's health care, it's essential to consult with your pediatrician and other healthcare providers to ensure safety and appropriateness. Discuss any concerns or questions you may have and work together to develop a comprehensive and individualized approach to your baby's health and wellness.

Conclusion

Nurturing your baby's health and wellness is a multifaceted journey that requires attention, care, and commitment. By scheduling well-baby checkups and vaccinations, recognizing signs of illness, practicing good hygiene, building a strong immune system, and exploring holistic approaches to healthcare, you'll create a foundation of health and wellness that supports your baby's growth and development.

Remember to trust your instincts as a parent and advocate for your baby's health and well-being. Stay informed, ask questions, and seek support when needed. Together with your pediatrician and healthcare team, you'll navigate the challenges and joys of parenthood with confidence and compassion, ensuring a bright and healthy future for your baby.

Chapter 07

Parenting as a Team

Parenthood is often described as a journey—a journey that's best undertaken together as a team. This chapter dives into the intricacies of parenting as a cohesive unit, emphasizing effective communication, fair distribution of responsibilities, nurturing your relationship amidst the demands of parenthood, resolving conflicts, making joint parenting decisions, and celebrating victories as a unified team.

Communicating Effectively with Your Partner

Effective communication serves as the bedrock of any successful partnership, especially in the context of parenting. Open, honest, and respectful communication between partners fosters understanding, trust, and unity in navigating the complexities of raising a child.

Active listening is a crucial component of effective communication. When your partner speaks, listen attentively, without interrupting or formulating a response before they've finished. Show empathy by acknowledging their feelings and validating their experiences, even if you don't necessarily agree with them.

Express yourself clearly and honestly, using "I" statements to convey your thoughts, feelings, and needs without placing blame on your partner. Avoid criticism, defensiveness, and contemptuous language, as these can escalate conflicts and undermine the foundation of your relationship.

Make time for regular check-ins with your partner to discuss parenting goals, challenges, and decisions. Set aside dedicated time each week to connect and communicate, whether it's during a quiet evening at home or a leisurely walk in the neighborhood.

Dividing Parenting Responsibilities Fairly

Balancing parenting responsibilities fairly ensures that both partners contribute equitably to the care and upbringing of their child. Recognize and appreciate each other's strengths, interests, and contributions as parents, and work collaboratively to divide tasks in a manner that feels balanced and manageable for both partners.

Start by discussing your individual strengths, preferences, and availability in terms of caregiving responsibilities. Consider factors such as work schedules, personal interests, and outside commitments when allocating tasks such as feeding, diapering, bathing, and bedtime routines.

Be flexible and willing to adjust roles and responsibilities as needed to accommodate changing circumstances and evolving needs. Remember that parenting responsibilities are not set in stone and may need to be renegotiated periodically to maintain fairness and balance.

Create a shared parenting calendar or schedule to keep track of responsibilities and appointments. Use a digital calendar or a physical planner to coordinate childcare duties, household chores, and other commitments, ensuring that both partners are on the same page and have a clear understanding of their responsibilities.

Nurturing Your Relationship Amidst Parenthood

Maintaining a strong and healthy relationship with your partner is essential for weathering the challenges of parenthood and preserving the bond that brought you together in the first place. Despite the demands of caring for a child, prioritize quality time together to nurture your connection and strengthen your partnership.

Schedule regular date nights or outings to reconnect and spend time together without the distractions of parenting. Whether it's a romantic dinner at a favorite restaurant, a leisurely stroll in the park, or a cozy movie night at home, prioritize uninterrupted time for just the two of you.

Find small ways to show appreciation and affection for your partner on a daily basis. Express gratitude for their contributions as a parent and partner, and acknowledge the value they bring to your family.

Communicate openly and honestly about your feelings,

needs, and concerns, and encourage your partner to do the same. Create a safe and supportive environment where you can share your thoughts and emotions without fear of judgment or criticism.

Resolving Conflicts and Making Parenting Decisions Together

Conflicts and disagreements are inevitable in any relationship, but learning to navigate them constructively is essential for maintaining harmony and unity in your parenting partnership. Approach conflicts as opportunities for growth and understanding, rather than as sources of contention or discord.

Practice active listening and empathy when resolving conflicts with your partner. Seek to understand their perspective and validate their feelings, even if you don't necessarily agree with them. Avoid blaming or criticizing your partner, and focus on finding mutually satisfactory solutions to the issue at hand.

When making parenting decisions, consider each partner's values, priorities, and parenting style. Take the time to discuss and explore different options, weighing the pros and cons together before reaching a decision that feels right for your family.

Be willing to compromise and make concessions when necessary, and prioritize the well-being and best interests of your child above all else. Remember that parenting is a shared responsibility, and decisions should be made collaboratively, with both partners having an equal voice in the process.

Celebrating Parenting Victories as a Team

Parenting is a journey filled with countless victories, both big and small, that deserve to be celebrated and cherished as a team. Take the time to acknowledge and appreciate the progress and achievements of your child, whether it's their first steps, first words, or academic accomplishments.

Celebrate your own accomplishments and milestones as parents, from surviving sleepless nights to mastering new parenting skills. Reflect on your journey together and take pride in the love, dedication, and resilience you've demonstrated as a team.

Find joy and fulfillment in the shared moments of laughter, learning, and growth that you experience as a family. Create lasting memories through shared experiences and traditions that strengthen your bond and bring you closer together.

Express gratitude and appreciation for your partner's contributions as a parent and partner, and acknowledge the value they bring to your family. Celebrate the victories, big and small, as a testament to your strength, resilience, and unwavering commitment to each other and to your child.

Conclusion

Parenting as a team requires dedication, communication, and collaboration. By communicating effectively with your partner, dividing parenting responsibilities fairly, nurturing your relationship amidst the demands of parenthood, resolving conflicts constructively, making joint parenting decisions, and celebrating victories as a unified team, you'll strengthen your bond as a couple and create a supportive and harmonious family environment for your child.

Remember that parenthood is a journey best undertaken together, with love, patience, and teamwork. Embrace the challenges and joys of parenting as opportunities for growth and connection, knowing that you and your partner are stronger together than apart. With open hearts and unwavering support for each other, you'll navigate the ups and downs of parenthood with grace and resilience, creating a lifetime of cherished memories and shared experiences along the way.

Chapter 08

Balancing Work and Family Life

Finding harmony between your career and family life is a common challenge for many parents. In this chapter, we'll explore strategies for planning parental leave, transitioning back to work, selecting quality childcare, managing work-life balance, coping with mom guilt, finding support in the workplace, and embracing the joys of parenthood while pursuing your career goals.

Planning for Parental Leave and Returning to Work

Planning for parental leave and transitioning back to work are significant milestones for new parents. Before your baby arrives, familiarize yourself with your employer's parental leave policies and consider how much time you'd like to take off to bond with your newborn.

Communicate with your employer early on to discuss your plans for parental leave and ensure a smooth transition back to work upon your return. Be proactive in arranging coverage for your responsibilities during your absence and providing clear instructions for your colleagues or temporary replacements.

Use your parental leave as an opportunity to focus on bonding with your baby, adjusting to your new role as a parent, and prioritizing self-care. Set realistic expectations for your return to work, allowing yourself time to readjust and transition back into your professional routine gradually.

Finding Quality Childcare Options

Finding quality childcare that meets your family's needs is essential for balancing work and family life. Start exploring childcare options well in advance of your return to work, considering factors such as location, cost, hours of operation, curriculum, and staff qualifications.

Research childcare providers in your area, including daycare centers, home-based daycares, nannies, and family childcare providers. Schedule visits to tour facilities, meet with providers, and ask questions about their programs, policies, and practices.

Consider seeking recommendations from other parents, friends, or coworkers who have experience with childcare providers in your area. Look for providers who are licensed, accredited, and have positive reviews from families they've served.

Trust your instincts and choose a childcare provider that aligns with your values, priorities, and preferences as a parent. Once you've selected a childcare arrangement, stay involved and engaged in your child's care, communicating regularly with your provider and staying informed about your child's experiences and development.

Managing Work-Life Balance: Setting Boundaries and Prioritizing

Maintaining a healthy work-life balance is essential for your overall well-being and happiness as a parent. Set clear boundaries between your work life and your family life, establishing dedicated time for both professional responsibilities and personal time with your loved ones.

Create a schedule or routine that allows you to allocate time and energy to work, family, self-care, and leisure activities. Prioritize tasks and responsibilities based on their importance and urgency, focusing on completing high-priority tasks during designated work hours and leaving non-urgent tasks for later.

Practice saying no to additional commitments or requests that don't align with your priorities or values. Learn to delegate tasks and responsibilities when necessary, both at work and at home, to lighten your workload and create more time for the things that matter most to you.

Set aside dedicated time for self-care and relaxation, whether it's engaging in hobbies, exercise, meditation, or spending quality time with your family. Prioritize activities that recharge your energy and nourish your soul, allowing you to show up as your best self in both your personal and professional life.

Coping with Mom Guilt and Finding Support in the Workplace

Mom guilt—a common phenomenon experienced by many working mothers—can arise from feelings of inadequacy, guilt, or anxiety about balancing work and family responsibilities. Recognize that mom guilt is a normal and natural response to the challenges of modern parenthood, and take steps to address and manage these feelings with compassion and self-care.

Practice self-compassion and forgiveness, recognizing that you're doing the best you can under the circumstances. Remind yourself that it's okay to prioritize your own needs and well-being, and that taking care of yourself allows you to better care for your family and excel in your career.

Seek support from your partner, friends, family members, and coworkers who understand and empathize with your experiences as a working parent. Connect with other working mothers through parent groups, online forums, or professional networks to share tips, advice, and encouragement.

Advocate for workplace policies and support systems that promote work-life balance and parental well-being, such as flexible work arrangements, parental leave policies, lactation support, and childcare assistance programs. Work with your employer to explore options for accommodations or adjustments that make it easier for you to balance your work and family responsibilities.

Embracing the Joys of Parenthood While Pursuing Career Goals

Despite the challenges of balancing work and family life, parenthood offers countless joys and rewards that enrich your life in profound ways. Embrace the unique experiences and moments of connection that parenthood brings, cherishing the precious time you spend with your child and the memories you create together.

Celebrate your successes and accomplishments as both a parent and a professional, recognizing the resilience, dedication, and love that you bring to both roles. Take pride in the positive impact you have on your child's life, nurturing their growth, development, and happiness with your unconditional love and support.

Find joy and fulfillment in pursuing your career goals and aspirations, knowing that your work not only provides for your family's financial security but also allows you to make a meaningful contribution to the world. Set ambitious yet achievable goals for yourself, and pursue them with passion, determination, and resilience.

Remember that parenthood is a journey, not a destination, and that each day presents new opportunities for growth, learning, and connection with your child. Embrace the challenges and triumphs of balancing work and family life with grace and resilience, knowing that you're capable of navigating this journey with love, courage, and determination.

Conclusion

Balancing work and family life is a complex and ongoing process that requires intention, prioritization, and flexibility. By planning for parental leave, finding quality childcare, managing work-life balance, coping with mom guilt, finding support in the workplace, and embracing the joys of parenthood while pursuing your career goals, you can create a fulfilling and harmonious life that honors both your professional aspirations and your commitment to your family.

Remember to prioritize self-care, seek support when needed, and celebrate the moments of connection, joy, and growth that parenthood brings. With love, resilience, and determination, you'll navigate the challenges of balancing work and family life with grace and confidence, creating a life that honors your values, priorities, and aspirations as a parent and a professional.

Chapter 09

Navigating Parenthood Challenges

Parenthood is a journey filled with joy, but it also comes with its fair share of challenges. This chapter delves into the intricacies of navigating common parenthood challenges, including dealing with parenting pressure and comparison, coping with unexpected surprises and changes, seeking support and resources, managing financial strain, and finding joy in the chaos of parenthood.

Dealing with Parenting Pressure and Comparison

Parenting pressure and comparison are pervasive in today's society, often exacerbated by social media, societal expectations, and well-meaning advice from family and friends. It's essential to recognize that every family is unique, and there's no one-size-fits-all approach to parenting.

Focus on your family's values, priorities, and goals, rather than comparing yourself to others. Remember that what works for one family may not work for another, and that's okay. Trust your instincts as a parent and make decisions that align with your values and beliefs.

Practice self-compassion and remind yourself that it's okay to make mistakes and learn as you go. Embrace the imperfections of parenthood and celebrate the unique qualities that make your family special.

Limit your exposure to social media and other sources of

pressure and comparison if they contribute to feelings of inadequacy or self-doubt. Surround yourself with supportive and understanding individuals who uplift and encourage you on your parenting journey.

Coping with Unexpected Parenthood Surprises and Changes

Parenthood is full of surprises and unexpected changes, from sleepless nights and developmental milestones to unexpected challenges and setbacks. Embrace the unpredictability of parenthood and approach each new experience with curiosity, flexibility, and resilience.

Accept that not everything will go according to plan, and that's okay. Embrace the spontaneity and unpredictability of parenthood, finding joy and humor in the unexpected twists and turns along the way.

Communicate openly with your partner about your feelings, concerns, and experiences as parents. Lean on each other for support and encouragement, and work together as a team to navigate unexpected surprises and changes.

Seek advice and guidance from trusted sources, such as pediatricians, parenting books, and online forums, when faced with unfamiliar or challenging situations. Remember that you're not alone, and there are resources and support available to help you navigate the ups and downs of parenthood.

Seeking Help and Resources: Support Groups and Counseling

Parenting can sometimes feel overwhelming, and it's okay to ask for help when you need it. Seek out support groups, parenting classes, and counseling services to connect with other parents and professionals who can offer guidance, encouragement, and practical advice.

Joining a support group or online community for parents allows you to share experiences, ask questions, and receive support from others who understand what you're going through. Hearing from others who have faced similar challenges can provide validation and reassurance that you're not alone.

Consider seeking individual or couples counseling if you're struggling with stress, anxiety, or relationship issues related to parenthood. A trained therapist can provide a safe and supportive space to explore your feelings, develop coping strategies, and strengthen your relationship with your partner.

Take advantage of parenting resources and programs offered by community organizations, healthcare providers, and educational institutions. Attend parenting classes, workshops, and seminars to learn new skills and strategies for managing common parenting challenges.

Managing Financial Strain and Budgeting for Parenthood

Parenthood often comes with financial challenges, from the cost of childcare and medical expenses to the need for larger living accommodations and additional expenses for baby supplies. Take proactive steps to manage financial strain and budget effectively for parenthood.

Create a realistic budget that accounts for all of your family's expenses, including housing, utilities, groceries, healthcare, childcare, and other essentials. Identify areas where you can cut back or reduce spending to free up resources for your growing family.

Start saving for parenthood as early as possible, setting aside money each month in a dedicated savings account or investment fund. Consider opening a college savings account for your child's education and contributing regularly to help prepare for future expenses.

Explore options for financial assistance, such as government programs, employer benefits, and community resources, that may help offset the cost of childcare, healthcare, and other expenses associated with parenthood.

Finding Joy in the Chaos: Embracing Imperfection and Learning from Mistakes

Parenthood is messy, chaotic, and unpredictable—but it's also incredibly rewarding and full of moments of joy and wonder. Embrace the imperfections of parenthood and focus on the moments of connection, love, and growth that make it all worthwhile.

Give yourself permission to let go of perfectionism and embrace the messy, imperfect reality of parenthood. Accept that mistakes will happen, and that's okay. Use each challenge and setback as an opportunity for growth and learning, both for yourself and your child.

Find joy in the small moments of everyday life, from cuddles and laughter to shared experiences and milestones. Cherish the memories you create with your child and celebrate the unique bond that you share.

Practice gratitude and mindfulness, taking time each day to reflect on the blessings and joys of parenthood. Focus on the present moment and savor the simple pleasures of spending time with your child, even amidst the chaos and challenges of daily life.

Conclusion

Parenthood is a journey filled with challenges, surprises, and unexpected twists and turns. By recognizing and addressing common parenthood challenges such as parenting pressure and comparison, unexpected surprises and changes, seeking support and resources, managing financial strain, and finding joy in the chaos of parenthood, you can navigate the ups and downs of parenthood with resilience, grace, and confidence.

Remember that you're not alone, and there are resources and support available to help you navigate the challenges of parenthood. Lean on your partner, family, friends, and community for support, and trust in your own abilities as a parent. With love, patience, and resilience, you'll navigate the joys and challenges of parenthood with grace and confidence, creating a lifetime of cherished memories and meaningful connections along the way.

Chapter 10

Celebrating Baby's First Year

Baby's first year marks a significant milestone not just for your little one but for your entire family. In this chapter, we'll delve into various ways to celebrate and cherish this special time, including reflecting on your parenting journey, planning your baby's first birthday celebration, creating time capsules and memory keepsakes, sharing your parenting wisdom with expectant parents, and embracing the adventure of parenthood beyond the first year.

Reflecting on Your Parenting Journey: Triumphs and Growth

As your baby completes their first year, take a moment to reflect on your parenting journey. Celebrate the triumphs, both big and small, that you and your baby have achieved together. Whether it's successfully navigating sleepless nights or witnessing your baby's first smile, each milestone is a testament to your love, dedication, and resilience as a parent.

Consider keeping a journal throughout your baby's first year to capture your thoughts, feelings, and experiences. Documenting the highs and lows of parenthood allows you to look back and appreciate the journey you've traveled together as a family.

Acknowledge the growth and transformation you've experienced as a parent over the past year. From mastering diaper changes to soothing your baby's cries, you've undoubtedly learned valuable skills and gained confidence in your ability to care for your little one.

Take pride in the bond you've formed with your baby, knowing that the love and connection you share will continue to deepen and evolve in the years to come. Parenthood is a journey of growth and discovery, and reflecting on your experiences helps you appreciate how far you've come.

Planning Baby's First Birthday Celebration

Your baby's first birthday is a momentous occasion that calls for a memorable celebration. Start planning early to ensure that the day is filled with joy, laughter, and special memories for your little one and your family.

Choose a theme for the birthday party that reflects your baby's personality and interests. Whether it's a favorite children's book, a beloved character, or a whimsical theme like a garden party or a circus extravaganza, let your creativity shine as you plan the decorations, activities, and menu.

Consider hosting the party at home or renting a venue that's suitable for young children. Outdoor parks, community centers, and play spaces offer ample room for little ones to explore and play, creating a fun and festive atmosphere for the celebration.

Plan age-appropriate activities and games to keep the little ones entertained. From a sensory play area and bubble station to a musical parade and storytelling corner, provide interactive experiences that engage your baby and their guests.

Capture the memories of your baby's first birthday celebration with photos, videos, and keepsakes that you can cherish for years to come. Consider hiring a professional photographer to document the special moments throughout the day, allowing you to focus on enjoying the festivities with your family and friends.

Creating Time Capsules and Memory Keepsakes

Create a time capsule or memory keepsake to commemorate your baby's first year and preserve precious memories for the future. Gather mementos and memorabilia from your baby's first year, such as photos, artwork, handprints, and keepsakes, and place them in a special container or memory box.

Include a letter to your baby, sharing your thoughts, hopes, and dreams for their future, as well as your reflections on their first year of life. Add small tokens and trinkets that hold sentimental value, such as a lock of hair, a hospital bracelet, or a favorite toy.

Store the time capsule or memory keepsake in a safe place where it can be easily accessed and enjoyed in the years to come. Consider revisiting the time capsule on your baby's future birthdays or significant milestones, reflecting on how much they've grown and changed over time.

Sharing Your Parenting Wisdom with Expectant Parents

As you reflect on your parenting journey and celebrate your baby's first year, consider sharing your wisdom and experiences with expectant parents who are embarking on their own journey into parenthood. Offer advice, encouragement, and support to help them navigate the challenges and joys of raising a child.

Share your favorite parenting tips and tricks, from soothing techniques and sleep solutions to feeding strategies and developmental milestones. Be honest and candid about the realities of parenthood, sharing both the joys and the challenges that come with caring for a baby.

Offer emotional support and reassurance to expectant parents, letting them know that it's okay to feel overwhelmed, anxious, or uncertain about becoming parents. Share your own experiences of overcoming obstacles and learning to trust your instincts as a parent, reassuring them that they're not alone on this journey.

Embracing the Adventure of Parenthood Beyond the First Year

As your baby's first year comes to a close, embrace the adventure of parenthood beyond the infancy stage. Look forward to the new experiences, milestones, and memories that await you and your growing family in the years to come.

Continue to nurture and support your child's development, fostering their curiosity, creativity, and independence as they explore the world around them. Embrace each new stage of childhood with enthusiasm and excitement, knowing that every phase brings its own unique joys and challenges.

Stay connected with other parents and caregivers in your community, sharing resources, advice, and support as you navigate the ups and downs of parenthood together. Lean on your support network for encouragement and guidance during times of uncertainty or difficulty, knowing that you're not alone on this journey.

Conclusion

Baby's first year is a time of incredible growth, love, and discovery for both parents and babies alike. By reflecting on your parenting journey, planning your baby's first birthday celebration, creating time capsules and memory keepsakes, sharing your parenting wisdom with expectant parents, and embracing the adventure of parenthood beyond the first year, you can celebrate this special milestone and look forward to the exciting journey ahead.

Remember to cherish each moment with your baby, knowing that the memories you create together will last a lifetime. Celebrate the triumphs, milestones, and memories of your baby's first year with love, gratitude, and joy, savoring the precious moments of parenthood that make it all worthwhile.

CONCLUSION

Congratulations! You've navigated through the whirlwind of baby's first year—a journey marked by growth, love, and countless precious moments. As you pause to reflect on this milestone, take pride in the journey you've embarked upon and the beautiful memories you've created along the way.

Reflecting on Your Parenting Journey

As you look back on the past year, take a moment to savor the milestones, both big and small, that have shaped your family's story. From the first time you held your baby in your arms to the late-night feedings and milestone moments, each experience has been a part of your parenting journey.

Celebrate the growth you've witnessed in your baby and in yourself as a parent. Recall the moments of joy, the challenges overcome, and the bonds strengthened as you navigated through the ups and downs of parenthood.

Embracing the Challenges and Joys of Parenthood

Parenthood is a journey filled with both challenges and joys, each one contributing to the tapestry of your family's life. Embrace the moments of uncertainty and doubt as opportunities for growth and resilience, knowing that you have the strength and determination to overcome any obstacle.

Find solace in the joyous moments of connection and love that parenthood brings. Whether it's a tender cuddle with your baby or a shared laugh with your partner, cherish these precious moments and hold them close to your heart.

Lean on your support system of family and friends during the challenging times, knowing that you are not alone on this journey. Seek comfort in the wisdom and guidance of fellow parents who understand the unique joys and struggles of raising a child.

Continuing to Learn and Grow as a Parent

As you celebrate the end of baby's first year, remember that your journey as a parent is far from over. Embrace the opportunity to continue learning and growing alongside your child, discovering new joys and navigating new challenges together.

Remain open to the lessons that parenthood teaches you, whether it's patience, resilience, or unconditional love. Embrace each new stage of your child's development with curiosity and enthusiasm, knowing that you have the power to shape their journey with love and intention.

Seek out resources and support to help you navigate the road ahead, whether it's parenting books, online communities, or the guidance of trusted professionals. Remember that there is no one-size-fits-all approach to parenting, and trust in your instincts to guide you on this incredible journey.

Wishing You a Lifetime of Love and Adventure with Your Little One!

As you embark on the journey beyond baby's first year, may your days be filled with endless love, laughter, and adventure with your little one by your side. Treasure each moment together, from the everyday routines to the special milestones, knowing that every moment is a precious gift.

Celebrate the unique bond that you share with your child, nurtured through love, patience, and unwavering dedication. Embrace the joy of parenthood and the beauty of watching your child grow and thrive in the world.

Congratulations once again on reaching this milestone in your parenting journey. Here's to many more years of love, laughter, and cherished memories with your growing family. Parenthood is an extraordinary adventure, and we wish you all the happiness and fulfillment that it brings. Cheers to the journey ahead!

Printed in Great Britain
by Amazon